C000142940

About this Learning Guide

Shmoop Will Make You a Better Lover*
*of Literature, History, Poetry, Life...

Our lively learning guides are written by experts and educators who want to show your brain a good time. Shmoop writers come primarily from Ph.D. programs at top universities, including Stanford, Harvard, and UC Berkeley.

Want more Shmoop? We cover literature, poetry, bestsellers, music, US history, civics, biographies (and the list keeps growing). Drop by our website to see the latest.

www.shmoop.com

Table of Contents

Introduction

In a Nutshell

Lord Tennyson became a very famous and popular poet over the course of his long career. He was the Poet Laureate of England for more than 40 years, from 1850 until he died in 1892. That means that, for most of the Victorian era, he was the most important and famous poet in England. So yeah, Tennyson was a big deal at a time when England itself was a pretty big deal.

But let's dial things back a little. "The Lady of Shalott" was an early work, written before Tennyson hit it big. He first published this poem in an 1833 book, and then again in a much more successful 1842 version. The version we use here is from 1842, and it's pretty different from the earlier one (you can check both of them out in our "Best of the Web" section). It's one of a few poems that he wrote about the legends of King Arthur. There have been a lot of books and poems written about Arthur and his knights, but Tennyson based his poem on an Italian book from the thirteenth century called *Donna di Scalotta*.

It was just the right moment for a work about King Arthur. In the Victorian Era the English were crazy for stories about Arthur, and this poem was embraced not just by readers but also by painters, who used it as inspiration for a bunch of famous paintings (see "Best of the Web" for some examples). In fact, people are still pretty nuts about this poem; it's got a blend of fantasy and tragedy that still fascinates readers, painters, musicians, etc. If you don't believe us, take a look at the web. We've picked some choice examples for you in "Best of the Web," but there's a world of "Lady of Shalott" stuff for you to explore out there. All that interest goes to show how popular this poem still is, more that 150 years after it was written.

Why Should I Care?

If you've watched *Lord of the Rings* or read *Harry Potter*, you really owe it to yourself to get to know "The Lady of Shalott." This poem is alive with the same sense of fantasy, adventure, and magic that you'll find in those works. Plus, this won't take you hours to get through. It's a compact and intense poem that manages to tell a big story in just over a hundred lines. "The Lady of Shalott" is exciting, sad, a little sexy, and plain old beautiful at the same time. We know that's a big sell for a little poem, but we're backed up by a whole bunch of "Lady of Shalott" fans, going back over more than 150 years. People have fallen in love with this poem over and over again, and it's inspired tons of paintings, songs, videos, etc. We're pretty sure that, once you dive into this poem, you'll see what all the fuss is about. This is the kind of poem that pulls you in fast and then sweeps you away. Have fun!

The Poem

Part I

On either side the river lie
Long fields of barley and of rye,
That clothe the wold and meet the sky;
And through the field the road runs by
To many-towered Camelot;
And up and down the people go,
Gazing where the lilies blow
Round an island there below,
The island of Shalott.

Willows whiten, aspens quiver,
Little breezes dusk and shiver
Through the wave that runs for ever
By the island in the river
Flowing down to Camelot.
Four grey walls, and four grey towers,
Overlook a space of flowers,
And the silent isle imbowers
The Lady of Shalott.

By the margin, willow-veiled,
Slide the heavy barges trailed
By slow horses; and unhailed
The shallop flitteth silken-sailed
Skimming down to Camelot:
But who hath seen her wave her hand?
Or at the casement seen her stand?
Or is she known in all the land,
The Lady of Shalott?

Only reapers, reaping early
In among the bearded barley,
Hear a song that echoes cheerly
From the river winding clearly,
Down to towered Camelot:
And by the moon the reaper weary,
Piling sheaves in uplands airy,
Listening, whispers "'Tis the fairy
Lady of Shalott."

Part II

There she weaves by night and day
A magic web with colours gay.
She has heard a whisper say,
A curse is on her if she stay
To look down to Camelot.
She knows not what the curse may be,
And so she weaveth steadily,
And little other care hath she,
The Lady of Shalott.

And moving through a mirror clear
That hangs before her all the year,
Shadows of the world appear.
There she sees the highway near
Winding down to Camelot:
There the river eddy whirls,
And there the surly village-churls,
And the red cloaks of market girls,
Pass onward from Shalott.

Sometimes a troop of damsels glad,
An abbot on an ambling pad,
Sometimes a curly shepherd-lad,
Or long-haired page in crimson clad,
Goes by to towered Camelot;
And sometimes through the mirror blue
The knights come riding two and two:
She hath no loyal knight and true,
The Lady of Shalott.

But in her web she still delights
To weave the mirror's magic sights,
For often through the silent nights
A funeral, with plumes and lights
And music, went to Camelot:
Or when the moon was overhead,
Came two young lovers lately wed;
"I am half sick of shadows," said
The Lady of Shalott.

Part III

A bow-shot from her bower-eaves,
He rode between the barley-sheaves,
The sun came dazzling through the leaves,

And flamed upon the brazen greaves
Of bold Sir Lancelot.
A red-cross knight for ever kneeled
To a lady in his shield,
That sparkled on the yellow field,
Beside remote Shalott.

The gemmy bridle glittered free,
Like to some branch of stars we see
Hung in the golden Galaxy.
The bridle bells rang merrily
As he rode down to Camelot:
And from his blazoned baldric slung
A mighty silver bugle hung,
And as he rode his armour rung,
Beside remote Shalott.

All in the blue unclouded weather
Thick-jewelled shone the saddle-leather,
The helmet and the helmet-feather
Burned like one burning flame together,
As he rode down to Camelot.
As often through the purple night,
Below the starry clusters bright,
Some bearded meteor, trailing light,
Moves over still Shalott.

His broad clear brow in sunlight glowed;
On burnished hooves his war-horse trode;
From underneath his helmet flowed
His coal-black curls as on he rode,
As he rode down to Camelot.
From the bank and from the river
He flashed into the crystal mirror,
"Tirra lirra," by the river
Sang Sir Lancelot.

She left the web, she left the loom,
She made three paces through the room,
She saw the water-lily bloom,
She saw the helmet and the plume,
She looked down to Camelot.
Out flew the web and floated wide;
The mirror cracked from side to side;
"The curse is come upon me," cried
The Lady of Shalott.

Part IV

In the stormy east-wind straining,
The pale yellow woods were waning,
The broad stream in his banks complaining,
Heavily the low sky raining
Over towered Camelot;
Down she came and found a boat
Beneath a willow left afloat,
And round about the prow she wrote
  The Lady of Shalott.

And down the river's dim expanse,
Like some bold seër in a trance
Seeing all his own mischance--
With a glassy countenance
Did she look to Camelot.
And at the closing of the day
She loosed the chain, and down she lay;
The broad stream bore her far away,
The Lady of Shalott.

Lying, robed in snowy white
That loosely flew to left and right--
The leaves upon her falling light--
Through the noises of the night
She floated down to Camelot:
And as the boat-head wound along
The willowy hills and fields among,
They heard her singing her last song,
The Lady of Shalott.

Heard a carol, mournful, holy,
Chanted loudly, chanted lowly,
Till her blood was frozen slowly,
And her eyes were darkened wholly,
Turned to towered Camelot.
For ere she reached upon the tide
The first house by the water-side,
Singing in her song she died,
The Lady of Shalott.

Under tower and balcony,
By garden-wall and gallery,
A gleaming shape she floated by,
Dead-pale between the houses high,
Silent into Camelot.

Out upon the wharfs they came,
Knight and burgher, lord and dame,
And round the prow they read her name,
  The Lady of Shalott.

Who is this? and what is here?
And in the lighted palace near
Died the sound of royal cheer;
And they crossed themselves for fear,
All the knights at Camelot:
But Lancelot mused a little space;
He said, "She has a lovely face;
God in his mercy lend her grace,
The Lady of Shalott."

Overview and Line-by-Line Summary

Brief Summary

This is a pretty long poem, and a lot goes on, but Tennyson makes it easier to follow along by breaking the action up into four parts. We'll take you through them quickly, to give you an overview:

Part 1: The poem opens with a description of a field by a river. There's a road running through the field that apparently leads to Camelot, the legendary castle of King Arthur. From the road you can see an island in the middle of the river called the Island of Shalott. On that island there is a little castle, which is the home of the mysterious Lady of Shalott. People pass by the island all the time, on boats and barges and on foot, but they never see the Lady. Occasionally, people working in the fields around the island will hear her singing an eerie song.

Part 2: Now we actually move inside the castle on the island, and Tennyson describes the Lady herself. First we learn that she spends her days weaving a magic web, and that she has been cursed, forbidden to look outside. So instead she watches the world go by in a magic mirror. She sees shadows of the men and women who pass on the road, and she weaves the things she sees into her web. We also learn that she is "half sick" of this life of watching and weaving.

Part 3: Now the big event: One day the studly Sir Lancelot rides by the island, covered in jewels and shining armor. Most of this chunk of the poem is spent describing Lancelot. When his image appears in the mirror, the Lady is so completely captivated that she breaks the rule and looks out her window on the real world. When she does this and catches a glimpse of Lancelot and Camelot, the magic mirror cracks, and she knows she's in trouble.

Part 4: Knowing that it's game over, the Lady finds a boat by the side of the river and writes her name on it. After looking at Camelot for a while she lies down in the boat and lets it slip downstream. She drifts down the river, singing her final song, and dies before she gets to

Camelot. The people of Camelot come out to see the body of the Lady and her boat, and are afraid. Lancelot also trots out, decides that she's pretty, and says a little prayer for her.

Part 1, Lines 1-10

Lines 1-5

On either side the river lie
Long fields of barley and of rye,
That clothe the wold and meet the sky;
And through the field the road runs by
To many-towered Camelot;

- Tennyson starts out this poem with a quiet description of a landscape. A river runs through fields of grain. The barley and the wheat cover ("clothe") the "wold" (an old word for an open, unforested piece of land). Through this field, there's a road running toward the castle of Camelot, which is the legendary home of King Arthur and his knights.

Lines 6-9

And up and down the people go,
Gazing where the lilies blow
Round an island there below,
The island of Shalott.

- Apparently this road is pretty well traveled. The people who use the road can look down and see an island in the middle of the river. This island, which the speaker says is surrounded by lilies, is called the island of Shalott.
- FYI, that's pronounced with the accent on the second syllable (sha-LOTT). To hear it out loud, check out one of the audio recordings of the poem in the "Best of the Web" section

Lines 10

Willows whiten, aspens quiver,

- The poem holds off on the plot details for a second here, and tells us a little more about the natural world around the island.
- We hear about the willow trees that grow on the river banks, and the aspen trees that "quiver" (when the wind blows though the branches of an aspen tree, the leaves shake or "quiver").

Part 1, Lines 11-23

Line 11
Little breezes dusk and shiver

- The speaker mentions little breezes that blow around the island too, and says that they "dusk and shiver." It's a little hard to say exactly what those words mean in this context, since we usually don't talk about something "dusking."
- All the same, can you feel the atmosphere this creates? Even if the words don't add up right away, can you feel the little chill of darkness and mystery they send through the line? That's what they're there for.

Lines 12-14
Through the wave that runs for ever
By the island in the river
Flowing down to Camelot.

- Those breezes run along with the river, which flows constantly past the island in an endless wave.
- Here the speaker is really underlining the flow of the river as it heads toward Camelot. That flow, that "wave that runs for ever" (line 12) will be really important later on, so he's careful to plant the idea in our heads now.

Lines 15-16
Four grey walls, and four grey towers,
Overlook a space of flowers,

- Now we hear about a building on the island, a simple structure, just four walls with four towers. We imagine a mini-castle, a way smaller version of the many-towered Camelot we heard about in line 5.
- It's apparently surrounded by flowers too. Weaving the natural and the manmade together is a big deal in this poem.

Lines 17-18
And the silent isle imbowers
The Lady of Shalott.

- Finally, we meet the star of this little show, the Lady herself. The only thing we learn right away is that the silent island of Shalott "imbowers" her. This might be an unfamiliar word,

but it's really important for this poem. It means to enclose, to shut up in a bower, which was the private room of a medieval lady. Right off the bat, we can feel how the lady is restricted, shut up, even imprisoned on this island.

Lines 19-23

By the margin, willow-veiled,
Slide the heavy barges trailed
By slow horses; and unhailed
The shallop flitteth silken-sailed
Skimming down to Camelot:

- Now we head back outside.
- The speaker is almost teasing us, giving us yet more descriptions of the banks of the river with its willow trees (fascinating, huh?).
- We also hear more about the traffic on the river. Horses pull big heavy barges upstream, and shallops (little open boats for shallow waters) fly ("flitteth") down the river to Camelot, pushed by their silky sails.

Part 1, Lines 23-41

Lines 24-27

But who hath seen her wave her hand?
Or at the casement seen her stand?
Or is she known in all the land,
The Lady of Shalott?

- Basically, lots of people pass up and down the river, traveling on it and using the path beside it.
- But has anyone, the speaker wonders, seen the Lady of Shalott wave her hand, or seen her standing at her window ("casement" is just an old-fashioned word for window)? In fact, he wonders, does anyone in the land know her at all? Apparently she's an invisible mystery, this lady.

Lines 28-32

Only reapers, reaping early In among the bearded barley,
Hear a song that echoes cheerly
From the river winding clearly,
Down to towered Camelot:

- It seems that only the people who gather the grain in the fields ("the reapers") notice a sign of the Lady. They hear her singing a song that echoes happily down the river to Camelot.
- Can you feel how everything pulls down toward Camelot? The fifth line in every stanza is (almost) always about something or someone going toward Camelot, like it was a magnet.

Lines 33-36

And by the moon the reaper weary,
Piling sheaves in uplands airy,
Listening, whispers "'Tis the fairy
Lady of Shalott."

- When the reapers are working at night, piling up "sheaves" (big bundles of cut grain), they hear the Lady singing. They seem a little enchanted/creeped out by her song, and call her "the fairy Lady of Shalott" as if she was a ghost or magical spirit.
- The first part ends, and we've still only heard about the Lady from a distance.

Part 2, Lines 37-50

Lines 37-38

There she weaves by night and day
A magic web with colours gay.

- If the Lady of Shalott never comes to the window, and no one ever sees her, what is the lady doing with her free time? She's weaving a "magic web" all day and all night. The speaker doesn't tell us right away what this web is, just that it's brightly colored.

Lines 39-41

She has heard a whisper say,
A curse is on her if she stay
To look down to Camelot.

- Why does she weave all the time without stopping? She's heard a rumor ("a whisper") that she'll be cursed if she should stop working ("stay" is an old way of saying stop or pause) and look down the river at Camelot.
- Think of the Lady like Sleeping Beauty in the Disney cartoon – a beautiful maiden, trapped in a tower under a terrible curse.

Lines 42-45

She knows not what the curse may be,
And so she weaveth steadily,
And little other care hath she,
The Lady of Shalott.

- The twist in this poem is that no one told the Lady of Shalott exactly what the curse involves. To be on the safe side, she just keeps weaving all the time, with nothing else ("little other care") to worry her or occupy her time – in other words, a pretty boring life.

Lines 46-50

And moving through a mirror clear
That hangs before her all the year,
Shadows of the world appear.
There she sees the highway near
Winding down to Camelot:

- The web she's weaving isn't the only magical prop in this poem. There's also a magic mirror, which shows "shadows of the world."
- That's an important phrase, and a little mysterious. She's not seeing the real thing, just images, and the use of the word "shadows" makes us think they might be fuzzy, dark, faint images. Still, this mirror gives her a way to watch the highway, even though she can't really look outside.

Part 2, Lines 51-41

Lines 51-54

There the river eddy whirls,
And there the surly village-churls,
And the red cloaks of market girls,
Pass onward from Shalott.

- What does she see on the highway in the mirror? For one thing, there's a spot in the river where the current makes a little whirlpool ("the river eddy whirls"). Mostly though, she sees a parade of people.
- The first people the speaker introduces to us are some rough peasants from the town ("surly village-churls") and some girls from the market in red cloaks.

Lines 55-59

Sometimes a troop of damsels glad,
An abbot on an ambling pad,
Sometimes a curly shepherd-lad,
Or long-haired page in crimson clad,
Goes by to towered Camelot;

- The parade of passers-by continues. We see a group of happy young women ("damsels glad"), then an abbot (the head of a monastery) on a lazy old horse ("an ambling pad"). Young men too, a shepherd with curly hair maybe, or a page (a young servant to a knight) with long hair and red clothes.
- We get lots of fun little details here, but these aren't really characters in the poem. They are meant to represent the outside world, the place where the Lady can't go.

Lines 60-63
And sometimes through the mirror blue
The knights come riding two and two:
She hath no loyal knight and true,
The Lady of Shalott.

- Sometimes, she sees knights in the mirror. This is a big deal because we know that knights are a major part of the Camelot story.
- The speaker notes that the Lady doesn't have a "loyal knight" of her own, and you can begin to feel her loneliness and longing. This is definitely a set-up for the rest of the poem.

Part 2, Lines 64-72

Lines 64-70
But in her web she still delights
To weave the mirror's magic sights,
For often through the silent nights
A funeral, with plumes and lights
And music, went to Camelot:
Or when the moon was overhead,
Came two young lovers lately wed;

- Whatever "magic sights" she sees in the mirror, the Lady weaves into her web.
- The speaker gives us a couple more examples of those magic sights: a funeral on a quiet night, full of light and music, or two newlyweds walking alone in the moonlight.

Lines 71-72

"I am half sick of shadows," said
The Lady of Shalott.

- Still, magic mirror or not, we get the sense that this is a pretty crummy deal for the Lady. She has some entertainment, but no real connection to the world. As she puts it: "I am half sick of shadows."
- She's fed up with this life, and we can feel that something may be about to change.

Part 3, Lines 73-81

Lines 73-74

A bow-shot from her bower-eaves,
He rode between the barley-sheaves,

- Here it comes – the big turn in this poem.
- Someone's coming, although in these lines, he's only identified as "He." He shows up riding through the barley just a "bow-shot" (as far as you could shoot an arrow) from the Lady's little prison.

Lines 75-76

The sun came dazzling through the leaves,
And flamed upon the brazen greaves

- Tennyson really ratchets up the effects for this big entrance. If it were a movie, this moment would definitely be in slow motion. The sun is dazzling and bright, and it sparkles off his greaves (that's a piece of armor, like metal shin-guards for a knight).

Line 77

Of bold Sir Lancelot.

- Then he drops the name. This isn't just any knight; it's Sir Lancelot, the toughest and most famous (and, we imagine, the best-looking) of King Arthur's Knights of the Round Table.
- Here's a note for all you poetry nerds: this is the only stanza where the fifth line doesn't end with the word "Camelot." Here it's "Lancelot," which is a sneaky but also maybe a really powerful way of showing how important he is.

Lines 78-79

A red-cross knight for ever kneeled
To a lady in his shield,

- Literally these lines mean that Lancelot's shield has a picture on it of a knight kneeling before his lady.
- Like in many spots in this poem, there's a lot more going on under the surface. The Redcross Knight is a character in *The Faerie Queene*, a famous epic poem by Edmund Spenser. The red cross is also the sign of St. George, the patron saint of England. Basically that picture on the shield is a symbol of courage, chivalry, and the political and literary history of England. You don't have to wrestle with all that stuff at once, but it's good to know that it's there.

Lines 80-81

That sparkled on the yellow field,
Beside remote Shalott.

- Check out how often the speaker reminds us where we are. Here he mentions the field of barley again, and the "remote" island of Shalott.
- It's pretty unlikely that you forgot about these natural details, so we think this has more to do with how Tennyson gives the poem its rhythm.

Part 3, Lines 82-90

Lines 82-84

The gemmy bridle glittered free,
Like to some branch of stars we see
Hung in the golden Galaxy.

- Brace yourself for a long description of Lancelot, with some unfamiliar words.
- This is the major shift in the plot, so the speaker has to get us really invested in Lancelot. He starts out by comparing his jewel-covered bridle (the gear that fits over the horse's head) to a constellation of stars in the sky.

Lines 85-86

The bridle bells rang merrily
As he rode down to Camelot:

- We also learn that the bridle has ringing bells on it, and that Lancelot is headed down the river, towards Camelot.

Lines 87-90

And from his blazoned baldric slung
A mighty silver bugle hung,
And as he rode his armour rung,
Beside remote Shalott.

- Lancelot apparently also has a strap or belt across his shoulder called a "baldric." It's specially decorated, or "blazon'd."
- Don't worry if these words are new to you. They would have seemed old-fashioned to readers in the nineteenth century too. Tennyson uses them to give this poem a medieval feel.
- The baldric was often used to carry something, and Lancelot is toting a silver bugle (a horn that a knight could blow in battle). All this gear is making a lot of noise as he heads down the trail.

Part 3, Lines 91-104

Lines 91-95

All in the blue unclouded weather
Thick-jewelled shone the saddle-leather,
The helmet and the helmet-feather
Burned like one burning flame together,
As he rode down to Camelot.

- There's more description here, of the jewels on his saddle, and his helmet, (with a feather sticking out of it) which burns like a flame.
- The take-away point here is that Lancelot is about as impressive, manly, and cool-looking as he could possibly be – sort of a medieval rockstar. Definitely the kind of guy a lonely lady could fall in love with.

Lines 96-99

As often through the purple night,
Below the starry clusters bright,
Some bearded meteor, trailing light,
Moves over still Shalott.

- Just for a little icing on the cake, the speaker compares Lancelot's feathered helmet to a shooting star, with a tail ("bearded") that lights up the night sky.

Lines 100-101

His broad clear brow in sunlight glowed;
On burnished hooves his war-horse trode;

- A few more lines describing the studly Lancelot: his forehead glows in the sunlight (which is apparently supposed to be sexy). His horse's hooves are polished ("burnished") and bright.

Lines 102-104

From underneath his helmet flowed
His coal-black curls as on he rode,
As he rode down to Camelot.

- He's even got great hair ("coal-black curls"), which flows out of his helmet. You should really be thinking of a movie star by now, some unbelievably cool, well-dressed dude. Shmoop won't pick one for you, since we don't know your type, but you get the idea, right?

Part 3, Lines 105-117

Line 105-106

From the bank and from the river
He flashed into the crystal mirror,

- Now he shows up in the Lady's "crystal mirror." She finally sees this superman we've already heard so much about, and we have to believe she's impressed.

Lines 107-108

"Tirra lirra," by the river
Sang Sir Lancelot.

- Lancelot is singing a song as he trots along, and we get a little snatch of it, just the words "Tirra Lirra."
- This may be a reference to Shakespeare's *The Winter's Tale* (Act 4, Scene 3) where one

of the characters sings a song about "The lark, that tirra-lirra chants." It's probably also just a nonsense word from an old song, like "hey nonny nonny" or "sha la la." It's important, however, because it echoes the Lady's singing from earlier in the poem.

Lines 109-113

She left the web, she left the loom,
She made three paces through the room,
She saw the water-lily bloom,
She saw the helmet and the plume,
She looked down to Camelot.

- When the Lady sees him, she makes a fateful choice. She steps away from her loom and walks across the room. For the first time she actually looks outside, and sees the real world, the lilies, the knight's helmet, and Camelot.
- The poem doesn't actually say that she's fallen hopelessly in love at the very sight of Lancelot, but that's pretty much the implication.

Lines 114-117

Out flew the web and floated wide;
The mirror cracked from side to side;
"The curse is come upon me," cried
The Lady of Shalott.

- Of course we learned early in the poem that the Lady is forbidden by the mysterious curse from looking outside. So when she does, her web flies apart and the magic mirror cracks.
- The Lady realizes right away that she's in trouble, and the third part of the poem finishes with her crying out: "The curse is come upon me."

Part 4, Lines 118-131

Lines 118-122

In the stormy east-wind straining,
The pale yellow woods were waning,
The broad stream in his banks complaining,
Heavily the low sky raining
Over towered Camelot;

- The weather lets us know that things are all messed up. There's a stormy wind, the leaves are yellow and fading ("waning"). Even the river "complains" and the sky is low and heavy

with rain above Camelot. The outside world reflects the Lady's sad situation.

Lines 123-126

Down she came and found a boat
Beneath a willow left afloat,
And round about the prow she wrote
The Lady of Shalott.

- Now the Lady does what pretty much everyone does when they feel bad: she goes and finds a boat and writes her name on it. Actually we're not sure why she does this, but it does make her easier to identify later in the poem.

Lines 127-131

And down the river's dim expanse,
Like some bold seër in a trance
Seeing all his own mischance--
With a glassy countenance
Did she look to Camelot.

- She doesn't get into the boat right away. Instead she hangs out for a moment and looks down the river.
- The speaker compares her to a seer (someone who can see the future) having a vision of his bad luck (mischance) in the future. She has a glazed expression ("glassy countenance") on her face. The Lady can sense already that she's doomed.

Part 4, Lines 132-144

Lines 132-135

And at the closing of the day
She loosed the chain, and down she lay;
The broad stream bore her far away,
The Lady of Shalott.

- Then, at the end of the day, the Lady undoes the chain that holds the boat to the shore, and lies down in the bottom of the boat. The river carries her away.

Lines 136-140

Lying, robed in snowy white

That loosely flew to left and right--
The leaves upon her falling light--
Through the noises of the night
She floated down to Camelot:

- This is one of the famous images from the poem, which you might have seen in paintings. The lady is dressed in loose white clothes that flap about her in the wind. Leaves fall on her lightly as she lies in the boat and drifts, through the night, down toward Camelot.

Lines 141-144
And as the boat-head wound along
The willowy hills and fields among,
They heard her singing her last song,
The Lady of Shalott.

- The boat heads slowly downstream, winding its way through the hills and fields. As it passes, people can hear the Lady singing her final song.
- In the movie version of this poem this would be the big tear-jerking scene, definitely in slo-mo, with a sad song by Enya or someone like that.
- The focus in this last part of the poem is very much on the sad and lonely fate of the Lady.

Part 4, Lines 145-153

Lines 145-146
Heard a carol, mournful, holy,
Chanted loudly, chanted lowly,

- The song she sings is haunting, sometimes soft, and sometimes loud.
- The poem's speaker really focuses his attention on this moment, helping us to imagine and almost hear the Lady's last song.

Lines 147-149
Till her blood was frozen slowly,
And her eyes were darkened wholly,
Turned to towered Camelot.

- Then, as she sings and floats, the lady starts to change. Her blood slowly freezes and her eyes grow dark.
- The poem doesn't come out and say it, but these must be the effects of the curse we've

heard so much about.

Lines 150-153

For ere she reached upon the tide
The first house by the water-side,
Singing in her song she died,
The Lady of Shalott.

- Here's the sad part. Before she reaches the first house in Camelot, the Lady of Shalott dies.
- The poem is careful to point out that she died singing, that her death and the end of her song were part of the same event.

Part 4, Lines 154-171

Lines 154-158

Under tower and balcony,
By garden-wall and gallery,
A gleaming shape she floated by,
Dead-pale between the houses high,
Silent into Camelot.

- Now, at last, we enter the city of Camelot that we've heard so much about.
- The lady floats by the towers, the gardens, and the houses of the town. She is described as a "gleaming shape," completely pale and cold. She is also silent; her song is over at last.
- The images in this last part of the poem are simple and clear, and that's part of their power.

Lines 159-162

Out upon the wharfs they came,
Knight and burgher, lord and dame,
And round the prow they read her name,
The Lady of Shalott.

- Everyone in the town comes out to see this sight. The people the speaker mentions are wealthy, noble people (a "burgher" was a wealthy man in a medieval town, usually a merchant or a businessman). They all crowd around by the river's edge and read the name written on the front of the boat.

Lines 163-167

Who is this? and what is here?
And in the lighted palace near
Died the sound of royal cheer;
And they crossed themselves for fear,
All the knights at Camelot:

- They have a lot of question about this mysterious sight. Who and what is this? It's a disturbing sight, and as the word gets out a party in the castle nearby quiets down. It's scary enough that even the famously brave knights of Camelot make the sign of the cross for protection.

Lines 168-171

But Lancelot mused a little space;
He said, "She has a lovely face;
God in his mercy lend her grace,
The Lady of Shalott."

- The poem closes with Lancelot's reaction to what he sees. He stops and thinks for a moment, and then declares that the lady is pretty. He also says a little prayer for her, hoping that God will have mercy and protect her now that she's passed on.
- This probably wasn't the meeting with Lancelot that the Lady was hoping for. In the end, he comes too late, and she

Technique

Symbols, Imagery, & Wordplay

Welcome to the land of symbols, imagery, and wordplay. Before you travel any further, please know that there may be some thorny academic terminology ahead. Never fear, Shmoop is here. Check out our "How to Read a Poem" section for a glossary of terms.

The River

This is the first big image in the poem, and it comes up again and again after the first line. It's almost like the backbone of the poem, running through it and holding it up. Do you feel how the river sort of pulls the plot along? That's especially true toward the end, as the Lady begins her final journey. The movement of the river, its flow and its strength, is so key to this poem that it's not surprising that Tennyson leads out with this image.

- Line 1: The river is the first image, and so, in a way, everything is put in relation to the river. Camelot is down the river, the island is in the middle of the river, the fields are on either

side of the river. Beginning, middle, and end, we keep coming back to the river.

- Line 13: In the line before this, the speaker has told us about the "wave that runs forever" down the river. We think this idea of an endless wave, a current that can't be stopped, is really key. The river is mostly peaceful and pretty, but there's something almost scary about this eternal wave. Finally, it's going to pull the Lady to her death.
- Line 120: As the situation with the Lady gets more serious, the river seems to pick up on her distress. In this line, we are told that the river is complaining. When you give human feelings to a non-human thing like a river, that's called **personification**. In this case it helps to emphasize the Lady's fate, which is apparently so tragic it can even make a river sad.

Camelot

Just the name of Camelot calls up **images** of amazing castles, kings and knights, and people living in peace and justice. Even in the fantasy world of this poem, it seems far away, untouchable until the very end. When we finally do see Camelot, it's a place of joy and beauty, every bit as social and splendid as the island of Shalott was lonely and sad.

- Line 5: We won't point out every spot where Camelot comes up, since the word is used as a **refrain** in the fifth line of almost every stanza. We think that repetition is meant to make Camelot seem more like a far off dream than an actual place. It's almost like heaven, a place the Lady can dream about but not actually see.
- Line 158: In this line, the Lady finally gets to Camelot, the place we've heard so much about. It's a place full of happy people, but for the Lady it's fatal. She can't enter the world of knights and ladies except as a pale and silent corpse in a coffin. When the lady arrives, she brings her sadness with her, and the appearance of her body kills the "royal cheer" of Camelot. It's a powerful image, almost like two worlds crashing together.

The Island

The island in the river, cut off from the land and the outside world, is a major **symbol** of the Lady's isolation and loneliness.

- Line 9: When we first hear about the island, in the middle of all that natural description, it sounds like kind of a nice spot, surrounded by flowers. It's a little isolated, sure, but maybe that's a good thing – it's peaceful, out of the way, off the beaten path, maybe the kind of place you'd like to have a cabin. It isn't until later that we learn about the sinister curse.
- Line 81: After the second stanza, the speaker actually doesn't use the word "island" again, but here he talks about "remote Shalott." That's an interesting phrase, and it shows how much our image of Shalott has changed. Now it seems lonely, and we know that, because of how remote the island is, the Lady will be separated from Lancelot as long as she stays there. The island has become like a prison, more like Alcatraz than some chilled-out little spot in the river.

The Lady of Shalott

Obviously she's the main character and a huge part of this poem, but is the Lady of Shalott a major **image**? Lancelot is almost buried in description, but we hear almost nothing about the Lady herself. Hair color, eyes, height? Those things aren't all crucial, but they'd help us to build a mental picture of our main character. In some ways, it feels like the speaker is trying to hold back an image of the Lady, to make her deliberately hard to imagine.

- Line 18: The first time we hear her name is as the closing line of the second stanza. We're going to hear the same thing a *lot* more before the poem is over. The Lady's name is a **refrain** that the speaker uses over and over. Her name almost starts to hypnotize us, like a magical spell.
- Line 71: Don't worry, we won't take you through all of the spots where the poem talks about the Lady, but we thought this one was worth mentioning. This is the place where the Lady admits her frustration with her life, and says she is "half sick of shadows." While we still don't get an image of her face, we can feel the strength of her personality in this moment, a glimmer of the independence and strong will that is about to blossom.
- Line 153: This is the end of the Lady's transformation, the moment of her death. She has moved from slavery and imprisonment to freedom, but it has cost her everything. Before she sang, now she is quiet. She was warm, now she is frozen. All of these are powerful **images** of loss and change. Eventually she becomes a sort of statue, a pale shape in a coffin-like boat.

The Magic Web

We think this is one of the most memorable and fascinating **images** in the poem. That's partly because of the use of the word "web." It must literally mean something like a tapestry, but when you hear that word, it's hard not to think of the lady as a kind of spider. There's some **irony** there though, because, while she seems to be in control, she's obviously caught in someone else's web. She should be the web-weaving predator, but instead she turns out to be the prey of some unseen, mysterious force.

- Line 38: Here's where we first hear about the web. This is a powerful image for a few reasons. First of all, it's just a really cool-sounding idea. We imagine the web having an enchanted life of its own, like the brooms in "The Sorcerer's Apprentice." At the same time, the theme of weaving is an **allusion** to older stories, in particular the *Odyssey*. In that famous epic poem, the hero's wife, Penelope, sits by herself and weaves while she waits for her husband to return.
- Line 64: This line takes a kind of different angle from the other references to the web. It mentions specifically that the Lady enjoys her weaving. Looked at in this way, the web seems more like an expression of her talent and creativity than a terrible curse. That's the neat thing about weaving in this poem. It could be a **symbol** of creative freedom and possibility, or a boring and endless chore, a symbol of slavery and imprisonment.
- Line 109: The first thing the lady does to break away from her prison is to step away from the loom, where she's weaving. It's just a few steps, but they have major consequences. The turn away from the web represents her refusal to be a slave, her decision to pursue love and the outside world, even if it means her death.
- Line 114: The web and the mirror are the main **symbols** of the Lady's weird pseudo-life on the island. So when the web flies apart here, we know that her island life is over and something else is starting. Still, since this is an image of destruction, we get a little hint of

her approaching doom.

The Mirror
This is the web's twin, the other half of the Lady's pair of magical props. Although the mirror brings the world to the Lady, it's nothing like the real thing. She sees images, shadows, a sort of half-world. It's like someone staying cooped up in her apartment watching TV for years. She'd know what was going on outside, but you couldn't really call that living could you? The Lady sees the world but she can't interact with it. In that way the mirror becomes another **symbol** of her intense, terrible isolation from the world.
- Line 46: Here's where the speaker introduces the mirror, which he calls a "mirror clear." Two lines later, he talks about how the mirror shows the "shadows of the world" (line 48). This idea of a clear mirror full of shadows is a bit of a **paradox**. How can something be shadowy and clear at the same time? It seems like the point here is that the mirror (like the web) is filled with bright colors and people of all kinds, but the Lady can tell that it isn't real. It doesn't have the intensity of real life; it's just a shadowy imitation.
- Line 65: The Lady's talent is that she can turn the sights of the mirror into an image in her web. It's because of this that we might think of the mirror and web as **metaphors** for the life of the artist. She can represent life, but she can't be a part of it. Artists, in a sense, are always taking a bird's-eye view, reproducing life from a distance. You can see how, if this went too far, it might make someone feel alienated and lonely and maybe even cursed like the Lady of Shalott. Maybe this poem is like a therapy session for Tennyson to gripe a little about his life.
- Line 106: The mirror, ironically, shows the Lady the thing that will break its spell over her. When Lancelot comes trotting into the mirror, everything changes for the Lady. Even a shadow of him in a mirror is enough to let her know she has to change her life. He must have been pretty hot. Seriously, would you risk your life for a reflection?

Sir Lancelot
We've said it before, but Lancelot is definitely the rockstar of this poem. Even in the Arthur legends, he has a reputation as an irresistible ladies' man. This poem spends a bunch of time letting us know how good he looks in his armor. Other than that, he doesn't have much to do – no dragons to slay or anything like that. All he has to do is show up and look good in a mirror, and he totally rocks the Lady of Shalott's world.
- Line 77: When he first shows up, he's gleaming in the sun, almost like he was on fire. To underline what a big event this is, Tennyson breaks a rule he keeps everywhere else in the poem. On this one occasion, instead of making "Camelot" the last word of the fifth line of the stanza, he uses "Lancelot" instead. It might not seem like a big deal, but it has a subtle effect, and it really points out how much the appearance of Lancelot shakes things up. The Lady's life is going to change completely.
- Line 82: In trying to capture the full awesomeness of Lancelot and his gear, the speaker uses a bunch of comparisons. In this case, he uses a **simile** to compare the horse's bridle, all covered in jewels, to a constellation of shining stars.
- Line 168: In Lancelot's last cameo appearance, we don't get as strong a visual image of

him. Still, this moment lets us see another side of him, and it's also where he says his only real line. At this point, instead of being a glittery piece of eye-candy, he seems sensitive and thoughtful. He's also gracious and thoughtful toward the dead Lady, showing that he's not just handsome but a class act too. He is, in the world of the poem, a perfect guy, bold, chivalrous, handsome, and kind.

Form and Meter

Rhyming Lines in Iambic and Trochaic Tetrameter

Let's start with the way Tennyson breaks up the lines in this poem. The most basic division in the poem is the four big chunks (Parts 1-4). It might help to think of these like acts in a play – they each focus on a different part of the plot. Part 1 describes the landscape around Shalott. Part 2 describes the Lady and the things she sees in her mirror. Part 3 deals with the appearance of Lancelot and how cool he is. Part 4 covers the Lady's boat ride and her death. When you move to a new part, it's a signal that the poem's plot is shifting gears.

The next important things to notice are the **stanzas**, the smaller groups of lines, which are like the paragraphs of a poem. In this particular poem, Tennyson makes it easy on us, because the stanzas are *always* nine lines long. There are a total of nineteen stanzas in the whole poem. If we count up the stanzas, we can see that the Parts of the poem get longer as we go along. The first two parts have four stanzas each, Part 3 has five stanzas, and Part 4 (the longest) has six stanzas. You definitely don't have to memorize these details, but it's good to keep an eye out for them. Great poems are always carefully put together.

Now let's check out the way this poem **rhymes**. Tennyson made a big deal out of the rhyming lines in this poem, which are super-noticeable once you start to focus on them. Each stanza in this poem rhymes in exactly the same way, so once we show you how one of them works, you'll know everything there is to know. We'll demonstrate with the first stanza. To make it clearer, we'll put rhyming sounds in bold, and give each different sound a letter:

On either side the river **lie A**
Long fields of barley and of **rye, A**
That clothe the wold and meet the **sky**; **A**
And through the field the road runs **by A**
To many-towered Came**lot; B**
And up and down the people **go, C**
Gazing where the lilies **blow C**
Round an island there **below, C**
The island of **Shalott. B**

See how that works? We start out with four rhyming lines in a row (in this case: lie, rye, sky, by). Then in line 5 we get the word "Camelot." The rhyme in this poem is so steady that the fifth line

of each stanza almost always ends with "Camelot." Then we get three more rhyming lines in a row (in this case go, blow, below). Finally, we end the stanza with the word "Shalott" which ends almost every stanza (and rhymes with "Camelot" in line 5). It might seem a little complicated at first, but like we say, once you have this down, it works for every stanza in the poem.

Finally, let's take a look at the rhythm of this poem (what English teachers call the **meter**). This one gets a little trickier than the rhyme. We won't bug you with all the details, but here's a quick overview:

Most of the lines in this poem have eight syllables, although there are a bunch with five or seven too. Tennyson uses two different basic rhythms for these lines. We'll show them to you so you can compare. Again, don't get freaked about these details, just think of them as a part of your poetry toolkit.

The first kind of meter is called **iambic**. In this meter, if you divide all the syllables in the line into groups of two, the emphasis falls on the second syllable (da DUM). That's how the poem starts out. We'll show you by dividing the syllables up with slashes and putting the stressed syllable in bold:

On **ei**|ther **side** | the **ri**|ver **lie**
Long **fields** | of **bar**|ley **and** | of **rye**,

Got that? Feel how the rhythm goes: da DUM da DUM da DUM da DUM? How about if we switch it around, and put the stress first? That's exactly what Tennyson does in the beginning of the second stanza:

Willows | **whi**ten,| **asp**ens | **qui**ver,
Little | **bree**zes | **dusk** and | **shi**ver

Feel the difference there? Now it goes: DUM da DUM da DUM da DUM da. We call this kind of meter **trochaic**. So in fancy English teacher terms, he's switched from iambic to trochaic tetrameter ("tetrameter" just means there are four groups of syllables per line). We're not so worried about the names, though. We just think it's worth tuning your ear a little so you can hear those shifts in rhythm. It's like learning to play your favorite song on a guitar. It helps you see how it's put together, and hopefully makes you love it even more.

Speaker

We never find out who put that curse on the Lady of Shalott. This made us a little bit curious. What if it turned out that it was the speaker of this poem? There are a lot of ways that you could picture the speaker of the poem, and we imagine an old witch telling this story, looking down into her crystal ball where she can see the images of the Lady and Lancelot.

Where do we get this? Well, there's the bird's-eye-view thing, right? This speaker sees and knows things no one else could. More than that, though, we think there's something a little cold in the sound of this speaker's voice, just a hint of pleasure at the way the Lady suffers, at the

irony of her last meeting with Lancelot. Plus, there's the way the speaker hides the details of the curse, almost like she was keeping a secret. Finally, isn't this whole poem a little like a magical spell, meant to draw you into this world and hold you there? The rhythm of the poem, the way we come back again and again to the same refrain – it's almost like we are being hypnotized, put under a curse ourselves by the sneaky magic of the speaker.

Sound Check

This poem is about a lady and a knight, for sure, but isn't it also about a river? Everything we see here – islands and trees and castle and fields – is stretched out along the river. It's like the poem's spine. We even think this poem sounds like a river. It burbles and swirls and gushes and roars like a river.

No really, think about it. A river doesn't just have one sound, it has many, and so does this poem. We start the poem with a quiet, lazy, open sound, like a river running flat and wide: "On either side the river lie/ Long fields of barley and of rye" (lines 1-2). Do you feel how relaxed and calm the river sound is here? No hurry, just smooth water and soft sounds.

Then in the next stanza, things start to pick up speed, and so does the sound. Now it's like a river rushing down the rapids: "Willows whiten, aspens quiver,/ Little breezes dusk and shiver" (lines 10-11). Can you hear how those words hurry and dance along the line? We're in a different part of the river, and the sound has changed completely.

The poem does this again, and again, speeding up, rushing and crashing, and then slowing down again, at the end of the stanza, where the short little refrain bubbles along: "The Lady of Shallot." See that? Just like a river, speeding up slowing down, loud, quiet, fast, slow, over and over.

What's Up With the Title?

On the surface, this is a pretty easy one. The Lady of Shalott is the heroine of the poem and the heroine of the title. Tennyson focuses us right away on the importance of the Lady. For all the poem has to say about Lancelot and Camelot, this is really her story.

For extra English lit. bonus points, we'll tell you that the Lady's name comes from the legend of Elaine of Astolat, a woman who died for the love of Lancelot. Tennyson changed her name to Shalott for this poem, and created a lot of the details himself.

Calling Card

Dramatic Subjects in Very Organized Poems

Tennyson had a long career (this is a pretty early poem), so he wrote a lot of different kinds of poetry after he finished with this King Arthur stuff. Still, he never got tried of big, dramatic, exciting stories. A lot of his poems deal with terrible grief, huge monsters, death-defying battles

and things like that. Still, he usually approaches those subjects in the same tight, controlled style you see here. The lines are short, the stanzas are regular, and the rhymes are carefully laid out. The emotions and the events are huge, but you never feel like the poem gets completely carried away by them.

Tough-O-Meter

(4) Base Camp
"The Lady of Shalott" tells a really great, engaging story, so that should make this climb exciting. Still, there's some tough vocab, and it's a pretty long climb, so it might take a little sweat to reach the top. It's worth it though, we promise!

Setting

The setting is like our world, only more so. Have you ever looked at something, and then put on a pair of sunglasses and looked again? You know how they can make something like a sunset seems more intense, brighter, more real than real? That's how we see the setting of this poem. It's not like you don't recognize the things you see, it's just that everything has been soaked in a weird and beautiful kind of magic. Things like trees that might ordinarily just stand there are suddenly almost alive; they dance and shiver. The river suddenly has a voice. It doesn't just burble along, it complains (line 120).

It's not like Tennyson just threw a few magic props into our world. There's something completely, mysteriously different about it. You imagine the sun would be brighter, the songs would be sweeter, and the knights would be taller and stronger. That magic mirror has a little bit of a "through-the-looking glass" feel to it already, and that's what we see everywhere around here: a world like ours, but a little distorted, richer and deeper and more fascinating.

Theme of Isolation
Whatever else the Lady of Shalott has going on, she's definitely alone. We don't know who shut her away in the castle or why, but it doesn't seem fair. We can tell that she's fed up with it; in fact she even says as much. Her desire to be part of the world, to interact, to love and be loved, is what pushes the whole plot of this poem. The fact that she never really breaks out of her loneliness is what gives "The Lady of Shalott" a tragic edge.

Questions About Isolation

1. Do you think the Lady of Shalott escapes her isolation by the end of the poem?
2. Does the magic mirror make her seem more isolated or less? Does that little bit of contact

with the world make things worse or better?

3. Is it better to die or to live the rest of your life alone? Do you think the Lady faces up to that choice? Does she basically commit suicide?
4. Do you think the fact that the lady spends her days working alone is a metaphor for the place of women in English society?

Chew on this: Isolation

The Lady of Shalott makes a confident choice to break free from her isolation. Although it costs her everything, it's still a strong and meaningful refusal of her shadowy, isolated situation.

The Lady of Shalott is engaged in lonely weaving, a traditional mode of women's labor. Her imprisoned isolation is a powerful metaphor for the social, sexual, and intellectual repression of women across English history.

Theme of Man and the Natural World

"The Lady of Shalott" is stuffed with references to the natural world. Tennyson loops back again and again to the fields and trees and flowers that surround the island of Shalott. In fact, you might get a little sick of hearing about it. Still, the movements of nature (especially the endless flowing of the river) are a big part of this poem's rhythm; they help it all hang together.

Questions About Man and the Natural World

1. What if you took all the stuff about flowers and islands and rivers out of this poem? Could you still tell this story?
2. Do you think the Lady misses contact with other people or with the natural world? Is it a little bit of both?
3. Is there a natural image from this poem that really sticks in your head? If so, what do you think makes it do that?
4. Is the Lady more a part of the human or the natural world?

Chew on this: Man and the Natural World

Finally, it is not just Lancelot that the Lady wants to be in contact with, but the flowers and the river and the leaves. She is a prisoner kept apart from nature as well as from her fellow humans.

The story of Lancelot and the Lady of Shalott is inseparable from the natural world. The river and its surroundings are a crucial focus of the entire poem and they give it its structure and rhythm.

Theme of Art and Culture

Although she's alone, and not too happy about it, the Lady of Shalott does have two things to keep her busy. She weaves and she sings. Even if no one sees her work, she's definitely an

artist. A lot of people read this whole poem as a metaphor for the lonely life of the artist. We'll definitely look at that possibility, but even without that big metaphor, we think the theme of art and artists is still a major part of "The Lady of Shalott."

Questions About Art and Culture

1. Does it make sense to call the Lady an artist? Do you have to be free in order to make art? What other terms might you use for her?
2. Some people think this poem is about the lonely life of the artist, shut away from the world. Does that make sense to you, or does it seem like making something out of nothing?
3. Both the Lady and Lancelot are singers. Does the poem treat their songs differently? Do we learn anything about them through their songs?
4. Is Lancelot, with all his shiny armor, jewels and painted shield, a kind of living work of art? How about the Lady with her name written on her boat, on display for the people of Camelot?

Chew on this: Art and Culture

The Lady, who spends her days trying to capture shadows, is a representative of all artists, who live partly in the living world and partly in a private dream.

By writing her name on her boat/coffin, the Lady of Shalott gives herself a title, making her death a work of art. This is a final act of confident self-definition, and proves that she is entirely free from her prison.

Theme of The Supernatural

The mysterious curse on the Lady of Shalott is a big part of the plot. It rules her life and causes her death. This little thread of black magic helps give "The Lady of Shalott" its spooky, sad atmosphere, and also connects it to the medieval fantasy world of wizards and spells. We can just tell that, if Tennyson were alive now, he'd be a huge Harry Potter fan.

Questions About The Supernatural

1. Why don't we learn more about the curse? Would the poem be better if it had more back-story, like a wicked queen who casts a spell or something like that?
2. Is the magic web meant to seem evil and scary, or is it a symbol of the Lady's power and skill?
3. Does all this stuff with magic spells and King Arthur seem a little nerdy to you? Do you kind of love it? Shmoop welcomes all poetry dorks. We understand, trust us.
4. The reapers call her the "fairy Lady of Shalott." Do you think she herself has magic powers, or is she just trapped by them?

Chew on this: The Supernatural

By eliminating specific information about the curse, Tennyson focuses our attention completely on the lady and her loneliness. This makes this primarily a human story with magic elements, rather than the other way around.

By associating the weaving of the Lady with magical power, the poem suggests that all art is a form of magic, a way of casting a spell.

Theme of Love

This is a tricky one, since no one in "The Lady of Shalott" admits to being in love. Still, the idea of love, even unspoken love, is so crucial to this entire plot. It's a really old story. Lancelot is the guy or girl you always wanted to talk to but never worked up the courage. Maybe you saw him across the lunchroom, but he never noticed you. Maybe she was in your math class but you never said hi. This is love from a distance, and it's real and raw and painful in this poem.

Questions About Love

1. Why doesn't the poem directly mention the Lady's love for Lancelot?
2. Do you think Lancelot falls in love with the Lady at the end? What does his final speech mean to you?
3. Would you call this a love story? What other names could you use for it? Basically, is love the most important theme here?
4. Did you ever risk anything major for love? Do you sympathize with the Lady's decision?

Chew on this: Love

This poem uses the love story as an excuse to explore a more powerful and crucial theme, the Lady's choice to set herself free, her refusal to be confined.

Although it's never explicitly stated, the poem suggests that Lancelot, in his way, is as isolated as the Lady, and as much in need of the connection and happiness that love could bring.

Isolation Quotes

And the silent isle imbowers
The Lady of Shalott. (lines 17-18)

Thought: We think this line really rides on that big vocab word: "imbowers." This means to close up in a bower, which is an old term that refers to a lady's private room. In another kind of poem, this could be associated with protection, keeping someone safe from the outside world. But in this poem, we think it's a lot darker than that. This bower is really a prison, even though we don't know who put it there. Even that bit about the "silent isle" emphasizes how lonely and

isolated and cut off from the world the Lady is.

She hath no loyal knight and true,
The Lady of Shalott. (lines 62-63)

Thought: She's not just isolated physically, but emotionally too. She wants what anyone wants, companionship, comfort, and love. She can see these things in her mirror, she can watch lovers stroll by, but she is cursed to be alone. That's what this line is all about. A knight, in this world, would protect and serve a lady, like the red-cross knight on Lancelot's shield (lines 78-9). In a sense the poem suggests that knights and ladies belong together, and a lady on her own is incomplete. You might have some problems with that idea, but that seems to be the message the Lady is getting.

"I am half sick of shadows," said
The Lady of Shalott. (lines 71-72)

Thought: Here's the clearest expression of frustration from the Lady. In this moment we learn not just that she feels isolated in her shadow world, but also that the isolation really hurts. She wants not only to watch other people but also to join them.

With a glassy countenance
Did she look to Camelot. (lines 130-131)

Thought: Sadly, even once she gets out of her prison/bower, the Lady is still isolated. We really feel it in this moment, as she looks down the river and sees her doom. She can feel the weight of the curse, and she knows she won't make it to Camelot, at least not alive. One of the things this poem might make us wonder is whether it's the physical isolation that's the problem or some kind of deeper loneliness inside. In general, the inside vs. the outside is a big and complicated theme in this poem.

Singing in her song she died, (line 152)

Thought: Ultimately, she dies alone. She might have achieved a kind of freedom at the end, but the Lady remains isolated through the whole poem. We get a lot of little hints about this. For example, she dies in a boat, which separates her from the river and the world – it's like a little coffin. Also, check out the way this line says she died "in" her song. That's a funny way of saying it, and gives us the feeling that she was somehow a prisoner in her lonely song too. Sorry, that sounds pretty grim doesn't it? This is not the happiest poem.

Man and the Natural World Quotes

On either side the river lie
Long fields of barley and of rye, (lines 1-2)

Thought: Opening lines are a big deal in any poem. They set the tone, and focus our attention on the first details. It's definitely no accident that this poem opens with a description of the landscape. This poem isn't just about what's happening, but *where* it's happening. We get a lot of detail about the natural world; we can almost see the golden grain and almost feel the tug of the river's current.

Willows whiten, aspens quiver,
Little breezes dusk and shiver (lines 10-11)

Thought: See what we mean about the importance of nature? These lines don't do a thing for the plot. They're almost like separate little nature poems in themselves, like a little haiku or something. Still, even if they seem separate from the story, they are full of life and movement and energy. In a way, they give an intensity and a rhythm to the larger poem. It's almost like the natural world is alive and singing in this moment. That's mostly thanks to the heavy meter. Hear it? WILL-ows WHI-ten, AS-pens QUI-ver. That, folks, is the magic of the trochee (see the "Form and Meter" section for more on that).

She saw the water-lily bloom, (line 111)

Thought: This is the moment when she looks out the window, the one thing she's not supposed to do. It's her moment of resistance, when she goes against the curse, whatever the consequences. The interesting thing here is that she doesn't just look at the studly Lancelot. She also looks at the blooming lilies. The natural world is part of what she's been missing. She wants contact with the handsome knight, but also with the blooming flowers.

In the stormy east-wind straining,
The pale yellow woods were waning, (lines 118-119)

Thought: At this point, the natural world starts to reflect the mood of the Lady and the atmosphere of the poem. As her danger increases, as she gets closer to her doom, the sky gets dark and heavy, and a storm blows up. Making the natural world reflect human moods is a pretty old poetic trick, and Tennyson goes all out with it here.

The leaves upon her falling light--
Through the noises of the night (lines 138-139)

Thought: Although she won't make it to Lancelot, she does make contact with the natural world. The river rocks her, the wind blows her clothes and the leaves cover her. Even this close to death, she is feeling a kind of freedom and movement that was never there before. The story of her human isolation is really tragic, but maybe her meeting with the natural world gives it a little bit of a silver lining.

Art and Culture Quotes

Hear a song that echoes cheerly (line 30)

Thought: On the face of it, this might not seem like it fits in the category of "art." Still, it's pretty clear that the Lady's song is something special. She isn't just humming here – when she sings, the people around her are enchanted. They stop and get quiet, as if she was casting a spell. It's the song that makes the reapers call her a "fairy" – one of a number of connections between art and magic. Plus it's her only way of communicating with the world, and that's a major function of art – it lets others know what's going on in your head.

There she weaves by night and day
A magic web with colours gay. (lines 37-38)

Thought: This is the clearest example of art in the poem. The Lady is, more than anything else, a weaver. She sits and weaves around the clock. From what we can tell, her weaving is beautiful. A lot of women in the Middle Ages probably would have done some weaving, but the "gay colors" of this magic web let us know that she isn't weaving something like clothes. Her work is designed to be beautiful.

But in her web she still delights
To weave the mirror's magic sights, (lines 64-65)

Thought: Another important side of the Lady's art is that it seems to make her happy. At least partly. It's a little bit of a contradiction. Here at least, she seems to really like weaving, turning what she sees in the mirror into something beautiful and permanent. Other lines, however, tell us that this isn't the whole story.

"I am half sick of shadows," said
The Lady of Shalott. (lines 71-72)

Thought: Here we see the dark side of the Lady's situation, and maybe of being an artist in general. If you grow beets or sell fish for a living, you are out in contact with the world and other people. Sure it's not as fancy as being an artist, but at least you're dealing with things that are definitely *real*. You can see how, if you were shut up in your room weaving, or painting, or writing poems (we're looking at you, Tennyson), you might get a little sick of it. Most artists aren't under a mysterious curse, but if you sit and write or weave long enough, you might start to feel like it.

And round about the prow she wrote
  The Lady of Shalott. (lines 125-126)

Thought: This is a weird moment, and there are all kinds of possible interpretations. Here's one: what if this writing on the boat is her way of turning herself into a work of art? Bear with us here. In general, you don't name your boat after yourself. It's just not something normal people do. So we think there must be something else going on here. Maybe this is the Lady's way of planting her flag in the world, of saying "I'm here, I exist, and my life is my art." She puts herself on display, in a way, for the people of Camelot, but especially for Lancelot. She becomes a work of art, a still life, framed by the boat in which she lies.

The Supernatural Quotes
Listening, whispers "'Tis the fairy
Lady of Shalott." (lines 35-36)

Thought: This is the first time the poem mentions anything magical or supernatural. The word fairy used to mean more than it usually does today. It wasn't just a little Tinkerbelle-like thing with wings. It meant a person or thing that was tied to the eerie supernatural forces of the world. These reapers are clearly meant to be superstitious townspeople, so it's hard to know how seriously to take them. Still, they raise a question that the poem never quite answers. Does the Lady of Shalott have magical powers herself, or is she just trapped by someone else's magic? Just something to think about.

A magic web with colours gay. (line 38)

Thought: This web and the mirror are the two big magic props in this poem. Were they put there by the person who cursed the Lady? Did she make them? We can't say for sure. In fact, the poem doesn't have much to say about any of its magical elements. It's all a bit mysterious, and that's kind of cool. If there was an obvious villain, it would be easy, but this way, we can't tell if the Lady is struggling against someone else, or herself.

She has heard a whisper say,
A curse is on her if she stay (lines 39-40)

Thought: No looking outside, just weaving. That's the rule. Kind of cruel and sad, but again, we don't know who to blame this on, since we don't really get any specifics on the curse. All the magic comes from a world of whispers and shadows, just a little hint of spooky mystery. It matters a ton for the plot of course, but Tennyson doesn't seem to want to get wrapped up in magical details.

The mirror cracked from side to side;
"The curse is come upon me," cried (lines 115-116)

Thought: Wham – there it goes. She slips up once, and looks outside, and the whole thing falls apart. She's cursed and doomed to die. Seems like the least fair punishment ever, especially with guys as hot as Lancelot wandering around. Still, even if it seems mysterious and bizarre, it's an intensely dramatic moment, really active and exciting.

Love Quotes

She hath no loyal knight and true,
The Lady of Shalott. (line 62-63)

Thought: This is pretty much the closest we're going to get to talking about love in this poem. Love is one of the big things missing in the Lady of Shalott's life. Maybe we aren't even really talking about romantic love here. Maybe she's missing something more like a companion. Maybe the "loyal knight and true" would be a boyfriend, or maybe he'd be more like a protector and partner.

A red-cross knight for ever kneeled
To a lady in his shield, (lines 78-79)

Thought: This is another version of the love or companionship that the lady can't have. This is a pretty old-fashioned idea of love, and it has everything to do with chivalry, and the way knights should behave toward ladies. It probably isn't much like our idea of boyfriend and girlfriend. Still, it's put in here to remind us of how little love the Lady has in her life. She and Lancelot cannot become the perfect knight and lady we see on Lancelot's shield.

From underneath his helmet flowed
His coal-black curls as on he rode, (lines 103-104)

Thought: If all the stuff about knights and ladies isn't necessarily about romantic love, this definitely is. Come on, "coal-black curls?" These are like lines from a romance novel. Tennyson is letting us know that Lancelot is hot, and that's all we need to know about these lines.

She left the web, she left the loom,
She made three paces through the room, (lines 109-110)

Thought: This is the sacrifice she makes for Lancelot and love. At least we think so. Is there any way to be sure that's why she defies the curse? Not as far as we can tell. She sees Lancelot and then she goes to the window. The events are really close, but neither she nor the speaker says a word about her falling in love. This is a pretty dramatic poem, but it also knows how to slow down when it need to, to keep things subtle instead of hitting you over the head with them.

The love plot is here, but it simmers under the surface.

He said, "She has a lovely face;
God in his mercy lend her grace, (lines 169-70)

Thought: Is Lancelot falling in love here too? It doesn't quite seem like that. It would be nice if he'd fall for her completely, but we just don't see it here. He acknowledges that she's pretty, but was that worth dying for? Still, there's a hint here, a little possibility that he understands what she's done for him. Not enough to take away the tragedy of the ending, but still, it's something.

Study Questions

1. Have you ever had a crush on someone who didn't know about it? Do you recognize any of the themes in this poem from your experience? Did you consider writing your name on a boat?
2. Alright, we'll go way out on a limb here, but do you think the Lady's lonely magic mirror could be compared to our TVs and computers? Do you buy the argument that technology makes us more isolated?
3. Do you think the ending of this poem is tragic? Is there another way to look at it? Is her death a kind of escape?
4. Do you think there's a message or a moral here? Why write this particular poem about this particular story? Don't worry, we won't quiz you on it – just something to think about.

Did You Know?

Trivia

- Tennyson composed many of his poems in his head, partly because he was extremely nearsighted. (Source)
- Lancelot was a way bigger jerk in the traditional legends of King Arthur. In those stories, Elaine of Astolat (after whom Tennyson modeled the Lady of Shalott) nurses him when he is sick. Then she tells him she loves him, and he turns her down. Heartbroken, she kills herself. On top of that, Lancelot sleeps with King Arthur's wife! Not such a noble knight after all. (Source)
- Tennyson wrote a 6000-line poem when he was twelve! We don't know about you, but we were proud that we'd memorized our multiplication tables at that age. (Source)

Steaminess Rating

PG

We think this poem's definitely got a romantic edge. Nothing too naughty, but if you didn't imagine the possibility of Lancelot and the Lady of Shalott getting together, you probably missed part of the fun.

Allusions and Cultural References

Literary References

- **Camelot**: This one you've probably heard of; it's famous for being the castle where the legendary King Arthur and his Knights of the Round Table lived. There are lots of legends about Arthur, written in several languages, and they give different details about Camelot. Maybe the most famous of the books about Arthur and Camelot is Thomas Malory's *Le Morte d'Arthur* (The Death of Arthur), written in the fifteenth century.
- **Lancelot**: Another big player in Arthurian legend. One of the most famous of Arthur's knights, he causes a bunch of trouble by sleeping with Queen Guinevere. Like we see in this poem, Lancelot seems to be trouble around the ladies. Again, he's a major character in Malory's *Morte d'Arthur*. That book tells one version of the story of Elaine of Astolat, who falls in love with Lancelot and then dies when he breaks her heart. If you want more info about Arthurian legend, we've posted some links in our "Best of the Web" section.
- **Red-Cross Knight**: Red-cross Knight is one of the heroes of Edmund Spenser's epic poem *The Faerie Queene*. "The Lady of Shalott" doesn't mention that character directly but it does talk about how Lancelot has a picture of "a red-cross knight" on his shield (line 78). Tennyson's readers would definitely have gotten the reference to Spenser. They would also have known that a red cross is the symbol of St. George, the patron saint of England. So this quick shout-out to the red-cross knight does a lot of work. It connects Lancelot with another great work of literature, but also with the idea of chivalry, bravery, and the history and glory of England.
- **"Tirra-Lirra"** : This weird little bit of a song is one of only two lines that Lancelot speaks in the whole poem. It's a reference to a song from Shakespeare's *The Winter's Tale* (Act 4, Scene 3) where one of the characters sings a song about "The lark, that tirra-lirra chants."

Best of the Web

Websites

A Side-by-Side Comparison of the Two Versions of the Poem

http://www.lib.rochester.edu/camelot/shalcomb.htm

Tennyson first published this poem in 1833. In 1842, he released a revised version of the poem. We used the 1842 version, but if you want a peek at the earlier one, here it is.

Lots of Good Material About the Poem

http://www.victorianweb.org/authors/tennyson/losov.html

There's a ton of info about "The Lady of Shalott" on the web. VictorianWeb.org is a good place to start, and they have especially good stuff about the relationship between this poem and the painters who were inspired by it.

King Arthur Info

http://www.lib.rochester.edu/camelot/mainmenu.htm

This site is packed with information and images about Arthurian legend, which is really vast and complicated, but also really important for this poem.

Video

Loreena McKennitt's "Lady of Shalott"

http://www.youtube.com/watch?v=MU_Tn-HxULM

A shorter version of the poem set to music by a Canadian singer who does a lot of Celtic stuff. It might be your style, or it might not, but it's definitely worth a look. As a bonus, it helped us to hear the rhythm of the poem.

Silent Film Interpretation of the Poem

http://www.youtube.com/watch?v=-Fw5xcDey2U

There are a *lot* of really crummy "Lady of Shalott" videos out there – trust us, we looked. This one, on the other hand, is pretty good, a simple and elegant take on the poem.

Audio

Reading by an English Actress

http://www.youtube.com/watch?v=bUuZBXNw0O8

Here's a reading of the poem by an English actress named Frances Jeater. See what you think of this one – we always think it's a good idea to listen to a few of these to get a feeling for the different choices a reader can make.

Another Reading

http://www.youtube.com/watch?v=aym_NBTLMSc

This has a gimmicky animated picture of Tennyson reading the poem. More importantly, though, it has a really classy English guy reading the poem.

Images

Super-Famous Painting of the Lady of Shalott

http://www.jwwaterhouse.com/view.cfm?recordid=28

The "Lady of Shalott" inspired a painting by John William Waterhouse that's just about as famous as the poem. If you've ever been to a college dorm, you've probably seen a poster of this hanging on someone's wall.

Out Flew the Web...

http://www.victorianweb.org/painting/whh/replete/P30.html

"The Lady of Shalott" was a really popular subject with Victorian painters. This painting shows the moment in the poem where the curse strikes the Lady of Shalott. If you look closely, you can see that her tapestry includes the Holy Grail, a huge part of Arthurian legend.

Another by Waterhouse

http://www.victorianweb.org/painting/jww/paintings/22.html

Here's another moment in the poem, showing the Lady bored and fed-up at her loom. Notice how different she looks in each painting – that's partly because the poem really says nothing about her physical appearance.

Shmoop's Poetry Primer

How to Read Poem

There's really only one reason that poetry has gotten a reputation for being so darned "difficult": it demands your full attention and won't settle for less. Unlike a novel, where you can drift in and out and still follow the plot, poems are generally shorter and more intense, with less of a conventional story to follow. If you don't make room for the *experience*, you probably won't have one.

But the rewards can be high. To make an analogy with rock and roll, it's the difference between a two and a half minute pop song with a hook that you get sick of after the third listen, and a slow-building tour de force that sounds fresh and different every time you hear it. Once you've gotten a taste of the really rich stuff, you just want to listen to it over and over again and figure out: how'd they do that?

Aside from its demands on your attention, there's nothing too tricky about reading a poem. Like anything, it's a matter of practice. But in case you haven't read much (or any) poetry before, we've put together a short list of tips that will make it a whole lot more enjoyable.

- **Follow Your Ears.** It's okay to ask, "What does it mean?" when reading a poem. But it's even better to ask, "How does it sound?" If all else fails, treat it like a song. Even if you can't understand a single thing about a poem's "subject" or "theme," you can always say something – anything – about the sound of the words. Does the poem move fast or slow? Does it sound awkward in sections or does it have an even flow? Do certain words stick out more than others? Trust your inner ear: if the poem sounds strange, it doesn't

mean you're reading it wrong. In fact, you probably just discovered one of the poem's secret tricks! If you get stuck at any point, just look for Shmoop's "Sound Check" section. We'll help you listen!

- **Read It Aloud.** OK, we're not saying you have to shout it from the rooftops. If you're embarrassed and want to lock yourself in the attic and read the poem in the faintest whisper possible, go ahead. Do whatever it takes, because reading even part of poem aloud can totally change your perspective on how it works.

- **Become an Archaeologist.** When you've drunk in the poem enough times, experiencing the sound and images found there, it is sometimes fun to switch gears and to become an archaeologist (you know -- someone who digs up the past and uncovers layers of history). Treat the poem like a room you have just entered. Perhaps it's a strange room that you've never seen before, filled with objects or people that you don't really recognize. Maybe you feel a bit like Alice in Wonderland. Assume your role as an archaeologist and take some measurements. What's the weather like? Are there people there? What kind of objects do you find? Are there more verbs than adjectives? Do you detect a rhythm? Can you hear music? Is there furniture? Are there portraits of past poets on the walls? Are there traces of other poems or historical references to be found? Check out Shmoop's "Setting," "Symbols, Imagery, Wordplay," and "Speaker" sections to help you get started.

- **Don't Skim.** Unlike the newspaper or a textbook, the point of poetry isn't to cram information into your brain. We can't repeat it enough: poetry is an experience. If you don't have the patience to get through a long poem, no worries, just start with a really short poem. Understanding poetry is like getting a suntan: you have to let it sink in. When you glance at Shmoop's "Detailed Summary," you'll see just how loaded each line of poetry can be.

- **Memorize!** "Memorize" is such a scary word, isn't it? It reminds us of multiplication tables. Maybe we should have said: "Tuck the poem into your snuggly memory-space." Or maybe not. At any rate, don't tax yourself: if you memorize one or two lines of a poem, or even just a single cool-sounding phrase, it will start to work on you in ways you didn't know possible. You'll be walking through the mall one day, and all of a sudden, you'll shout, "I get it!" Just not too loud, or you'll get mall security on your case.

- **Be Patient.** You can't really understand a poem that you've only read once. You just can't. So if you don't get it, set the poem aside and come back to it later. And by "later" we mean days, months, or even years. Don't rush it. It's a much bigger accomplishment to actually *enjoy* a poem than it is to be able to explain every line of it. Treat the first reading as an investment – your effort might not pay off until well into the future, but when it does, it will totally be worth it. Trust us.

- **Read in Crazy Places.** Just like music, the experience of poetry changes depending on your mood and the environment. Read in as many different places as possible: at the beach, on a mountain, in the subway. Sometimes all it takes is a change of scenery for a poem to really come alive.

- **Think Like a Poet.** Here's a fun exercise. Go through the poem one line at a time, covering up the next line with your hand so you can't see it. Put yourself in the poet's shoes: If I had to write a line to come after this line, what would I put? If you start to think like this, you'll be able to appreciate all the different choices that go into making a poem. It can also be pretty humbling – at least we think so. Shmoop's "Calling Card" section will help you become acquainted with a poet's particular, unique style. Soon, you'll be able to

The Lady of Shalott
Shmoop Poetry Guide

decipher a T.S. Elliot poem from a Wallace Stevens poem, sight unseen. Everyone will be so jealous.

- **"Look Who's Talking."** Ask the most basic questions possible of the poem. Two of the most important are: "Who's talking?" and "Who are they talking to?" If it's a Shakespeare sonnet, don't just assume that the speaker is Shakespeare. The speaker of every poem is kind of fictional creation, and so is the audience. Ask yourself: what would it be like to meet this person? What would they look like? What's their "deal," anyway? Shmoop will help you get to know a poem's speaker through the "Speaker" section found in each study guide.
- And, most importantly, **Never Be Intimidated.** Regardless of what your experience with poetry in the classroom has been, no poet wants to make his or her audience feel stupid. It's just not good business, if you know what we mean. Sure, there might be tricky parts, but it's not like you're trying to unlock the secrets of the universe. Heck, if you want to ignore the "meaning" entirely, then go ahead. Why not?   If you're still feeling a little timid, let Shmoop's "Why Should I Care" section help you realize just how much you have to bring to the poetry table.

Poetry is about freedom and exposing yourself to new things. In fact, if you find yourself stuck in a poem, just remember that the poet, 9 times out of 10, was a bit of a rebel and was trying to make his friends look at life in a completely different way. Find your inner rebel too. There isn't a single poem out there that's "too difficult" to try out – right now, today. So hop to it. As you'll discover here at Shmoop, there's plenty to choose from.

Sources:

http://allpoetry.com/column/2339540
http://academic.reed.edu/writing/paper_help/figurative_language.html
http://web.uvic.ca/wguide/Pages/LiteraryTermsTOC.html#RhetLang
http://www.tnellen.com/cybereng/lit_terms/allegory.html

What is Poetry?

What is poetry? At the most basic level, poetry is an *experience* produced by two elements of language: "sense" and "sound." The "sense" of a word is its meaning. The word "cat" refers to a small, furry animal with whiskers, a long tail, and, if you're unlucky, a knack for scratching up all your new furniture. We can all agree that's what "cat" means. But "cat" also has a particular sound when you say it, and this sound is different from similar words for "cat" in other languages.

Most of the things that you hear, say, or read in your daily life (including the words you are reading right now) put more emphasis on meaning than on sound. Not so with poetry. Have you ever repeated a word so many times that it started to sound strange and foreign? No? Try saying that word "cat" twenty times in a row. "Cat, cat, cat, cat, cat, cat . . ." Kind of weird,

right? Well, guess what: you just made poetry out of a single word – that is, you turned the word into an experience that is as much about sound as it is about sense. Congratulations, poet!

Or let's imagine that you type the words "blue" and "ocean" on a page all by their lonesome selves. These two little words are quite ordinary and pop up in conversations all the time. However, when we see them isolated, all alone on a page, they might just take on a whole new meaning. Maybe "blue ocean" looks like a little strand of islands in a big sea of white space, and maybe we start to think about just how big the ocean is. Or you could reverse the order and type the words as "ocean blue," which would bring up a slightly different set of connotations, such as everyone's favorite grade-school rhyme: "In 1492 Columbus sailed the ocean blue."

Poetry is also visual, and so it's a good idea to pay attention to how the words are assembled on the page. Our imaginations are often stirred by a poem's visual presentation. Just like a person, poems can send all kinds of signals with their physical appearance. Some are like a slick businessman in a suit or a woman in an evening gown. Their lines are all regularized and divided neatly into even stanzas. Others are like a person at a rock concert who is dressed in tattered jeans, a ragged t-shirt, and a Mohawk, and who has tattoos and piercings all over their body! And some poems, well, some poems look like a baked potato that exploded in your microwave. It's always a good idea to ask yourself how the appearance of words on the page interacts with the meaning of those words. If the poem is about war, maybe it looks like a battle is going on, and the words are fighting for space. If the poem is about love, maybe the lines are spaced to appear as though they are dancing with one another. Often the appearance and meaning will be in total contrast, which is just as interesting.

OK, that's a very broad idea of what poetry is. Let's narrow it down a bit. When most people talk about poetry, they are talking about a particular kind of literature that is broken up into lines, or *verses*. In fact, for most of history, works divided into verse were considered more "literary" than works in prose. Even those long stories called "epics," like Homer's *The Odyssey* and Virgil's *Aeneid*, are actually poems.

Now, you're thinking: "Wait a minute, I thought verses belong to songs and music." Exactly. The very first poets – from Biblical times and even before – set their poems to music, and it's still acceptable to refer to a poem as a "song." For example, the most famous work by the American poet Walt Whitman is titled, "Song of Myself." Because of their shared emphasis on sound, poetry and music have always been like blood brothers.

The last thing to say about poetry is that it doesn't like to be pinned down. That's why there's no single definition that fits all of the things that we would call "poems." Just when you think you have poetry cornered, and you're ready to define it as literature broken into lines, it breaks free and shouts, "Aha! You forgot about the *prose poem*, which doesn't have any verses!" Drats! Fortunately, we get the last laugh, because we can enjoy and recognize poems even without a perfect definition of what poetry is.

Sources:

http://allpoetry.com/column/2339540

http://academic.reed.edu/writing/paper_help/figurative_language.html
http://web.uvic.ca/wguide/Pages/LiteraryTermsTOC.html#RhetLang
http://www.tnellen.com/cybereng/lit_terms/allegory.html

Poetry Glossary

Allegory: An allegory is a kind of extended metaphor (a metaphor that weaves throughout the poem) in which objects, persons, and actions stand for another meaning.

Alliteration: Alliteration happens when words that begin with the same sound are placed close to one another. For example, "the **s**illy **s**nake **s**ilently **s**linked by" is a form of alliteration. Try saying that ten times fast.

Allusion: An allusion happens when a speaker or character makes a brief and casual reference to a famous historical or literary figure or event.

Anaphora: Anaphora involves the repetition of the same word or group of words at the beginning of successive clauses or sections. Think of an annoying kid on a road trip: "Are we there yet? / Are we going to stop soon? / Are we having lunch soon?". Not a poem we'd like to read in its entirety, but the repetition of the word "are" is anaphora.

Anthologize: To put in a poetry anthology, usually for teaching purposes, so that students have a broad selection of works to choose from. Usually, the word will come up in a context like this: "That's one of her most famous poems. I've seen it anthologized a lot." An anthology is a book that has samples of the work of a lot of different writers. It's like a plate of appetizers so you can try out a bunch of stuff. You can also find anthologies for different periods, like Romantic, Modern, and Postmodern. The Norton, Columbia, and Best American anthologies are three of the most famous.

Apostrophe: Apostrophe is when an idea, person, object, or absent being is addressed as if it or they were present, alive, and kicking. John Donne uses apostrophe when he writes this: "Death be not proud, though some have called thee / Mighty and dreadful."

Avant Garde: You'll hear this word used to describe some of the craziest, most far-out, experimental poets. It was originally a French expression that refers to the soldiers who go explore a territory before the main army comes in. Avant garde artists are often people who break through boundaries and do what's never been done before. Then again, sometimes there's a good reason why something has been done before…

Ballad: A ballad is a song: think boy bands and chest-thumping emotion. But in poetry, a ballad is ancient form of storytelling. In the (very) old days, common people didn't get their stories from books – they were sung as musical poems. Because they are meant to convey information, ballads usually have a simple rhythm and a consistent rhyme scheme. They often tell the story of everyday heroes, and some poets, like Bob Dylan, continue to set them to

music.

Blank Verse: Thanks to Shakespeare and others, blank verse is one of the most common forms of English poetry. It's verse that has no rhyme scheme but has a regular meter. Usually this meter is iambic pentameter (check out our definition below). Why is blank verse so common in English? Well, a lot of people think we speak in it in our everyday conversations. Kind of like we just did: "a LOT of PEO-ple THINK we SPEAK in IT." That could be a blank verse line.

Cadence: Cadence refers to the rhythmic or musical elements of a poem. You can think of it as the thing that makes poetry sound like poetry. Whereas "meter" refers to the regular elements of rhythm – the beats or accents – "cadence" refers to the momentary variations in rhythm, like when a line speeds up or slows down. Poets often repeat or contrast certain cadences to create a more interesting sound than normal prose.

Caesura: A fancy word for a pause that occurs in the middle of a line of verse. Use this if want to sound smart, but we think "pause" is just fine. You can create pauses in a lot of ways, but the most obvious is to use punctuation like a period, comma, or semicolon. Note that a pause at the end of a line is not a caesura.

Chiasmus: Chiasmus consists of two parallel phrases in which corresponding words or phrases are placed in the opposite order: "Fair is foul, foul is fair."

Cliché: Clichés are phrases or expressions that are used so much in everyday life, that people roll their eyes when they hear them. For example, "dead as a doornail" is a cliché. In good poetry, clichés are never used with a straight face, so if you see one, consider why the speaker might be using it.

Concrete Poetry: Concrete poetry conveys meaning by how it looks on the page. It's not a super-accurate term, and it can refer to a lot of different kinds of poems. One classic example is poems that look like they thing they describe. The French poet Guillaume Apollinaire wrote a poem about Paris in the shape of the Eiffel tower.

Connotation: The suggestive meaning of a word – the associations it brings up. The reason it's not polite to call a mentally-handicapped person "retarded" is that the word has a *negative* connotation. Connotations depend a lot on the culture and experience of the person reading the word. For some people, the word "liberal" has a positive connotation. For others, it's negative. Think of connotation as the murky haze hanging around the literal meaning of a word. Trying to figure out connotations of words can be one of the most confusing and fascinating aspects of reading poetry.

Contradiction: Two statements that don't seem to agree with each other. "I get sober when I drink alcohol" is a contradiction. Some contradictions, like "paradox" (see our definition below), are only apparent, and they become true when you think about them in a certain way.

Denotation: The literal, straightforward meaning of a word. It's "dictionary definition." The word "cat" denotes an animal with four legs and a habit of coughing up furballs.

Dramatic Monologue: You can think of a dramatic monologue in poetry as a speech taken from a play that was never written. Okay, maybe that's confusing. It's a poem written in the voice of a fictional character and delivered to a fictional listener, instead of in the voice of a poet to his or her readers. The British poet Robert Browning is one of the most famous writers of dramatic monologues. They are "dramatic" because they can be acted out, just like a play, and they are monologues because they consist of just one person speaking to another person, just as a "dialogue" consists of two people speaking. (The prefix "mono" means "one," whereas "di" means "two").

Elegy: An elegy is a poem about a dead person or thing. Whenever you see a poem with the title, "In Memory of . . .", for example, you're talking about an elegy. Kind of like that two-line poem you wrote for your pet rabbit Bubbles when you were five years old. Poor, poor Bubbles.

Ellipsis: You see ellipses all the time, usually in the form of "…". An ellipsis involves leaving out or suppressing words. It's like . . . well, you get the idea.

Enjambment: When a phrase carries over a line-break without a major pause. In French, the word means, "straddling," which we think is a perfect way to envision an enjambed line. Here's an example of enjambment from a poem by Joyce Kilmer: 'I think that I shall never see / A poem as lovely as a tree." The sentence continues right over the break with only a slight pause.

Extended metaphor: A central metaphor that acts like an "umbrella" to connect other metaphors or comparisons within it. It can span several lines or an entire poem. When one of Shakespeare's characters delivers an entire speech about how all the world is a stage and people are just actors, that's extended metaphor, with the idea of "theater" being the umbrella connecting everything.

Foot: The most basic unit of a poem's meter, a foot is a combination of long and short syllables. There are all kinds of different feet, such as "LONG-short" and "short-short-LONG." The first three words of the famous holiday poem, "'Twas the Night before Christmas," are one metrical foot (short-short-LONG). By far the most important foot to know is the iamb: short-LONG. An iamb is like one heartbeat: ba-DUM.

Free Verse: "Free bird! Play free bird!" Oops, we meant "Free verse! Define free verse!" Free verse is a poetic style that lacks a regular meter or rhyme scheme. This may sound like free verse has no style at all, but usually there is some recognizable consistency to the writer's use of rhythm. Walt Whitman was one of the pioneers of free verse, and nobody ever had trouble identifying a Whitman poem.

Haiku: A poetic form invented by the Japanese. In English, the haiku has three sections with five syllables, seven syllables, and five syllables respectively. They often describe natural imagery and include a word that reveals the season in which the poem is set. Aside from its three sections, the haiku also traditionally features a sharp contrast between two ideas or images.

Heroic Couplet: Heroic couplets are rhyming pairs of verse in iambic pentameter. What on earth did this "couplets" do to become "heroic"? Did they pull a cat out of a tree or save an old

lady from a burning building? In fact, no. They are called "heroic" because in the old days of English poetry they were used to talk about the trials and adventures of heroes. Although heroic couplets totally ruled the poetry scene for a long time, especially in the 17th and 18th centuries, nowadays they can sound kind of old-fashioned.

Hyperbole: A hyperbole is a gross exaggeration. For example, "tons of money" is a hyperbole.

Iambic Pentameter: Here it is, folks. Probably the single most useful technical term in poetry. Let's break it down: an "iamb" is an unaccented syllable followed by an accented one. "Penta" means "five," and "meter" refers to a regular rhythmic pattern. So "iambic pentameter" is a kind of *rhythmic pattern* that consist of *five iambs* per line. It's the most common rhythm in English poetry and sounds like five heartbeats: ba-DUM, ba-DUM, ba-DUM, ba-DUM, ba-DUM. Let's try it out on the first line of Shakespeare's *Romeo and Juliet*: "In fair Verona, where we lay our scene." Every second syllable is accented, so this is classic iambic pentameter.

Imagery: Imagery is intense, descriptive language in a poem that helps to trigger our senses and our memories when we read it.

Irony: Irony involves saying one thing while really meaning another, contradictory thing.

Metaphor: A metaphor happens when one thing is described as being another thing. "You're a toad!" is a metaphor – although not a very nice one. And metaphor is different from simile because it leaves out the words "like" or "as." For example, a simile would be, "You're *like* a toad."

Metonymy: Metonymy happens when some attribute of what is being described is used to indicate some other attribute. When talking about the power of a king, for example, one may instead say "the crown"-- that is, the physical attribute that is usually identified with royalty and power.

Ode: A poem written in praise or celebration of a person, thing, or event. Odes have been written about everything from famous battles and lofty emotions to family pets and household appliances. What would you write an ode about?

Onomatopoeia: Besides being a really fun word to say aloud, onomatopoeia refers either to words that resemble in sound what they represent. For example, do you hear the hissing noise when you say the word "hiss" aloud? And the old Batman television show *loved* onomatopoeia: "Bam! Pow! Kaplow!"

Oxymoron: An oxymoron is the combination of two terms ordinarily seen as opposites. For example, "terribly good" is an oxymoron.

Paradox: A statement that contradicts itself and nonetheless seems true. It's a paradox when John Donne writes, "Death, thou shalt die," because he's using "death" in two different senses. A more everyday example might be, "Nobody goes to the restaurant because it's too

crowded."

Parallelism: Parallelism happens a lot in poetry. It is the similarity of structure in a pair or series of related words, phrases, or clauses. Julius Caesar's famous words, "I came, I saw, I conquered," are an example of parallelism. Each clause begins with "I" and ends with a verb.

Pastoral: A poem about nature or simple, country life. If the poem you're reading features babbling brooks, gently swaying trees, hidden valleys, rustic haystacks, and sweetly singing maidens, you're probably dealing with a pastoral. The oldest English pastoral poems were written about the English countryside, but there are plenty of pastorals about the American landscape, too.

Personification: Personification involves giving human traits (qualities, feelings, action, or characteristics) to non-living objects (things, colors, qualities, or ideas).

Pun: A pun is a play on words. Puns show us the multiple meanings of a word by replacing that word with another that is similar in sound but has a very different meaning. For example, "when Shmoop went trick-or-treating in a Batman costume, he got lots of snickers." Hehe.

Quatrain: A stanza with four lines. Quatrains are the most common stanza form.

Refrain: A refrain is a regularly recurring phrase or verse especially at the end of each stanza or division of a poem or song. For example in T.S. Eliot's *Love Song for J. Alfred Prufrock*, the line, "in the room the women come and go / Talking of Michelangelo" is a refrain.

Rhetorical Question: Rhetorical questions involve asking a question for a purpose other than obtaining the information requested. For example, when we ask, "Shmoop, are you nuts?", we are mainly expressing our belief that Shmoop is crazy. In this case, we don't really expect Shmoop to tell us whether or not they are nuts.

Rhyming Couplet: A rhyming couplet is a pair of verses that rhyme. It's the simplest and most common rhyme scheme, but it can have more complicated variations (see "Heroic Couplet" for one example).

Simile: Similes compare one thing directly to another. For example, "My love is like a burning flame" is a simile. You can quickly identify similes when you see the words "like" or "as" used, as in "x is like y." Similes are different from metaphors – for example, a metaphor would refer to "the burning flame of my love."

Slam: A form of contemporary poetry that is meant to be performed at informal competitions rather than read. Slam readings are often very political in nature and draw heavily from the rhythms and energy of hip-hop music.

Slant Rhyme: A rhyme that isn't quite a rhyme. The words "dear" and "door" form a slant rhyme. The words sound similar, but they aren't close enough to make a full rhyme.

Sonnet: A well-known poetic form. Two of the most famous examples are the sonnets of

William Shakespeare and John Donne. A traditional sonnet has fourteen lines in iambic pentameter and a regular rhyme scheme. Sonnets also feature a "turn" somewhere in the middle, where the poem takes a new direction or changes its argument in some way. This change can be subtle or really obvious. Although we English-speaking folks would love to take credit fort this amazing form, it was actually developed by the Italians and didn't arrive in England until the 16th century.

Speaker: The speaker is the voice *behind* the poem – the person we imagine to be speaking. It's important to note that the speaker is *not* the poet. Even if the poem is biographical, you should treat the speaker as a fictional creation, because the writer is choosing what to say about himself. Besides, even poets don't speak in poetry in their everyday lives – although it would be cool if they did.

Stanza: A division within a poem where a group of lines are formed into a unit. The word "stanza" comes from the Italian word for "room." Just like a room, a poetic stanza is set apart on a page by four "walls" of blank, white space.

Symbol: Generally speaking, a symbol is a sign representing something other than itself.

Synecdoche: In synecdoche a part of something represents the whole. For example: "One does not live by bread alone." The statement assumes that bread is representative of all categories of food.

Syntax: In technical terms, syntax is the study of how to put sentences together. In poetry, "syntax" refers to the way words and phrases relate to each other. Some poems have a syntax similar to everyday prose of spoken English (like the sentences you're reading right now). Other poems have a crazier syntax, where it's hard to see how things fit together at all. It can refer to the order of words in a sentence, like Yoda's wild syntax from the *Star Wars* movies: "A very important concept in poetry, syntax is!" Or, more figuratively, it can refer to the organization of ideas or topics in a poem: "Why did the poet go from talking about his mother to a description of an ostrich?"

Understatement: An understatement seeks to express a thought or impression by underemphasizing the extent to which a statement may be true. Understatement is the opposite of hyperbole and is frequently used for its comedic value in articles, speeches, etc. when issues of great importance are being discussed. Ex: "There's just one, tiny, little problem with that plan – it'll get us all killed!"

Sources:

http://allpoetry.com/column/2339540
http://academic.reed.edu/writing/paper_help/figurative_language.html
http://web.uvic.ca/wguide/Pages/LiteraryTermsTOC.html#RhetLang
http://www.tnellen.com/cybereng/lit_terms/allegory.html

Printed in Great Britain
by Amazon

85618974R00032